Construction

From Creating Early Shelters to Building a Sustainable Future

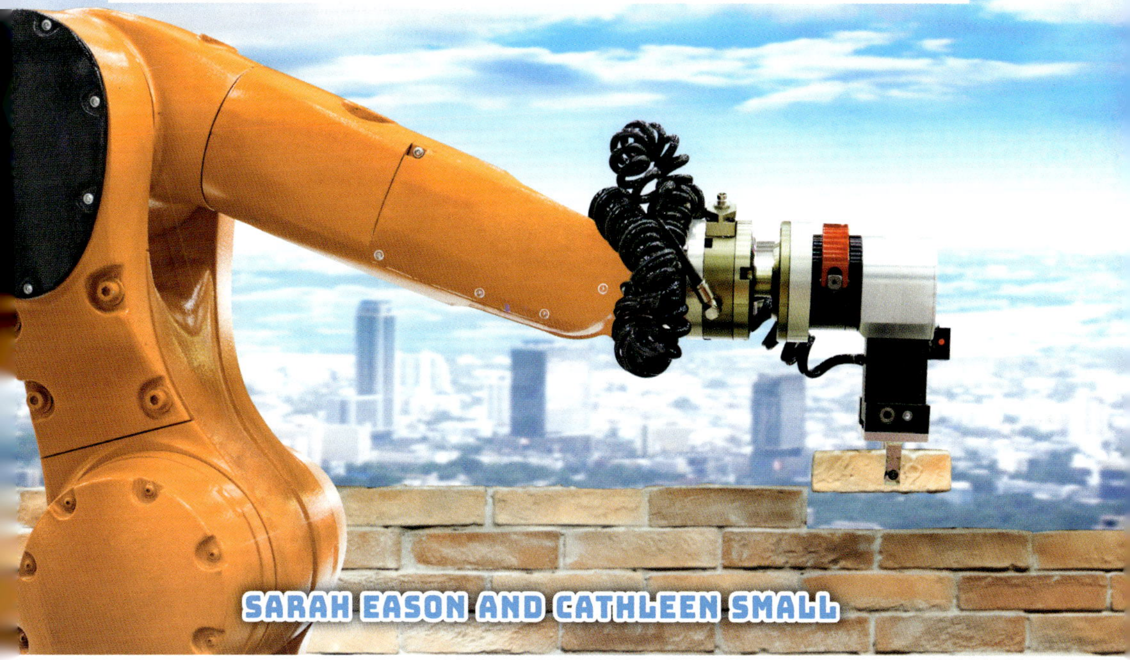

SARAH EASON AND CATHLEEN SMALL

Published in 2026 by Cheriton Children's Books
1 Bank Drive West, Shrewsbury, Shropshire, SY3 9DJ, UK

First Edition

Authors: Sarah Eason and Cathleen Small
Editor: Jennifer Sanderson
Designer: Paul Myerscough
Proofreader: Ellie Truman

Picture credits: Cover: Shutterstock/Dreamer Company (left), Shutterstock/giocalde (right). Inside: p1: Shutterstock/Engineer Studio, p4: Shutterstock/Gorodenkoff, p5: Shutterstock/Ryan DeBerardinis, p6: Shutterstock/Olya Maximenko, p7: Shutterstock/Chepesch, p8: Shutterstock/Azer Mess, p9: Shutterstock/Fabiano Goreme Caddeo, p10: Shutterstock/Blaz Kure, p11: Shutterstock/FrentaN, p12c: Shutterstock/AI Generator, p12b: Shutterstock/Walencienne, p14: Shutterstock/E-lona, p15: Shutterstock/Saravutpics, p16: Shutterstock/Photocreo Michal Bednarek, p17: Shutterstock/Nicholas Courtney, p18: Shutterstock/Tarcisio Schnaider, p19: Shutterstock/Corona Borealis Studio, p20b: Shutterstock/Leszek Glasner, p20t: Shutterstock/Body Stock, p21: Shutterstock/Creative Travel Projects, p22t: Shutterstock/Laurello, p22c: Shutterstock/Laurello, p22b: Shutterstock/Laurello, p24: Shutterstock/Photoongraphy, p25: Shutterstock/Alexanderstock23, p26: Shutterstock/Kristin Spalder, p27: Shutterstock/Lzf, p28t: Shutterstock/Jm13129, p28bl: Shutterstock/UsamaManzoor, p28br: Shutterstock/Fuyu Liu, p30: Shutterstock/Dagmara K, p31: Shutterstock/Frantic00, p32t: Shutterstock/Robert Kneschke, p32b: Shutterstock/Fotogrin, p34: Shutterstock/XSLT Studio, p35c: Shutterstock/Sergey Kolesnikov, p35b: Shutterstock/DC Studio, p36t: Shutterstock/Artie Medvedev, p36b: Shutterstock/R Nagy, p38: Shutterstock/Larisa Rudenko, p39: Shutterstock/Kaninw, p40c: Shutterstock/Shigemi Okano, p40b: Shutterstock/F11photo, p41: Shutterstock/Tong Stocker, p42b: Shutterstock/Andrew Will, p42c: Shutterstock/Vvaldmann, p43: Shutterstock/GoodMan Ekim, p44: Shutterstock/Zhu Difeng, p45: Shutterstock/Irene Miller, p46: Shutterstock/BearFotos, p47: Shutterstock/Attasit Saentep, p48: Shutterstock/Titov Dmitriy, p49: Shutterstock/Richard OD, p50t: Shutterstock/Rawpixels Stock, p50b: Shutterstock/Solar Energy, p52: Shutterstock/Ethan Daniels, p53t: Shutterstock/Petair, p53br: Shutterstock/FotoKina, p54c: Shutterstock/Flying a Hippo, p54b: Shutterstock/Andrew Angelov, p55: Shutterstock/Engineer Studio, p56: Shutterstock/Amorn Suriyan, p57: Shutterstock/FOTO Eak, p58: Shutterstock/BigPixel Photo.

Printed in China

Please visit our website,
www.cheritonchildrensbooks.com
to see more of our high-quality books.

CONTENTS

EVOLUTIONS IN ENGINEERING

Engineering is the use of scientific, mathematical, and practical ideas to design and create things such as buildings, machines, and devices to solve problems and improve people's lives. The people who come up with ideas for these buildings, machines, and devices are engineers. We have engineers to thank for the many innovations in building science that have happened throughout the ages, from shelters that evolved from simple tents to more permanent structures and modern skyscrapers.

The Story of Construction

In early times, buildings served one simple purpose: to shelter people from weather and environmental dangers such as wild animals. They were usually temporary because early civilizations were largely nomadic. This meant the people moved around. However, as civilizations began to focus on agriculture, shelters became more permanent, and eventually buildings moved from being structures designed just to protect people to buildings designed for certain purposes. That included buildings for sleeping, buildings for cooking, and buildings in which communities could meet. Today, we have buildings for a wide variety of uses—and their designs and structures are often shaped around their intended use.

Caves were used as a place of shelter for hunter-gatherers. Early people made paintings on the cave wall showing scenes from their lives.

When you look at a city full of skyscrapers, you'll see a world of construction engineering feats.

Engineering Past, Present, and Future

One of the main challenges engineers involved in buildings face is space. In places where a lot of people want to live there is usually little space. For example, large cities can quickly run out of space for buildings. That is because a lot of people move to cities for job opportunities. Cities also have things people need and like, such as restaurants and stores. However, most cities are limited in geographical area. For example, San Francisco covers just under 47 square miles (121 sq km) and New York City covers 302 square miles (783 sq km). While those areas sound large, they are not when you think about how many people use the area.

Engineering has helped us create tall buildings and skyscrapers that can expand upward rather than outward. And engineers will continue to help us build. But they will do so with creative ideas that make the most efficient use of the space they have and with less impact on the environment. As populations grow, we will continue to face a lack of space for building. We will also need to consider the natural resources we use for building, which are not limitless. The engineers of tomorrow will need to put all their creative skills to work to find solutions to these challenges.

An Engineering Evolution

In this book, we'll explore great feats of construction engineering through history, from earliest times to the present day. We'll discover how engineering has evolved and how ancient engineering has inspired modern engineering. We'll learn how engineers have come up with resourceful ways to solve our current building issues. We'll also explore the exciting developments in engineering that are just around the corner for the construction industry, and discover how they could provide the answer to our future needs.

CHAPTER 1

THE HISTORY OF BUILDING AND ENGINEERING

To understand the engineering evolutions in building, it helps to look at the history of construction. By looking at ancient societies and their practices, we can learn what drove the earliest innovations and how we went from the simple shelters of ancient times to the towering, impressive buildings of today.

The Earliest Shelters

The earliest examples of buildings were the shelters that nomadic people used in the late Stone Age (around 8000–4000 BCE). At that time, people were hunter-gatherers who moved from place to place in search of food and water. Sometimes, they sought shelter in caves but often, they constructed temporary shelters. The first records of such shelters are from before 12000 BCE, when it appears people made circular rings of stones. It is thought that they used poles made from wood to which skins of animals were attached to make tents. A basic level of structural engineering was needed to create these shelters. The poles and rocks needed to be placed in such a manner that the skins would be held down as "walls." Those walls protected people inside the tents from wind, rain, snow, and extreme heat.

Settling and Setting up Home

In around 10000 BCE, the hunter-gatherers turned to agricultural practices and became more stationary. Instead of moving about in search of food, they set up more permanent shelters and began to farm. This led to some of the first building engineering innovations.

This is a replica of an early human shelter.

BIG Breakthroughs

The pole, rock, and skin dwellings people had been making up until 10000 BCE were not strong enough for longer-term use. To overcome this problem, ancient people created tholoi. These were dwellings that involved basic masonry, using stone or clay to build walls. Both were more weather-resistant than the animal skins used previously. Archeologists have found evidence of tholoi villages in the Middle East and Europe. The earliest tholoi were circular in structure, with domed roofs—a little like the igloo dwellings used by the Inuit.

HOW IT WORKS:
A THOLOS

Tholoi are buildings with a basic circular igloo-type shape. A single building of this type is called a tholos. The structure of a tholos is simple but these buildings were surprisingly sturdy. This is how they were made:

1. A single circle of stones, clay blocks, or bricks is laid out.
2. A second layer of stones is placed on top of the first layer but with a slightly smaller diameter than the first layer.
3. A third layer of stones is put on top of the second layer but again with a slightly smaller diameter.
4. The process is repeated with each layer slightly smaller in diameter than the one below it. This means that the building becomes narrower as it approaches the top.

These ruins of tholoi were found in Greece. They show how a tholos was circular in shape.

Timber Makes an Appearance

Wood was used to make the sturdy poles used in the earliest structures. However, it was not until the Neolithic period (which started in around 7000 BCE) that heavier timber was used for building. At that time, tools were very basic so cutting down trees was difficult. However, there are some examples of timber structures from then: Neolithic long houses were built in Europe in around 6000 BCE. They were usually 18 to 23 feet (5.5 to 7 m) wide and 66 to 148 feet (20 to 45 m) long.

Neolithic builders also used timber to construct rectangular dwelling frames that had poles and columns sunk into the ground for stability. This system is similar to that used in modern buildings. The poles were anchored to the ground through an underground foundation and load-bearing walls. When tools developed and it became easier to cut timber, wood became more commonly used, and structures began to look more like the buildings we know today.

BIG Breakthroughs

The pitched roof was a breakthrough during the Neolithic period. Neolithic builders used thatch for roofs. Thatch is dried grass. However, builders quickly learned that such roofs leaked in the rain. They needed a way to get the rain to run off the roof, rather than leak through it. So they came up with the idea of angled, or pitched, roofs to encourage water runoff. This roof style is still used today for many structures, such as houses. In areas where there is heavy snowfall, it is common for a roof to be even more steeply pitched than in areas that have less severe weather.

Thatched roofs, like this one, were common in structures during the Neolithic period.

ENGINEERING EVOLUTIONS

Discover how timber engineering has evolved from ancient times to today in chapter 2. →

Bricks on the Scene

The Bronze Age started in around 3300 BCE, and during this time the first cities sprang up. They formed in the river valleys of Africa and Asia. The river valleys were rich with clay that could be found on the riverbanks. People used this clay to make bricks.

The first bricks were dried in the sun. The Mesopotamians soon applied their pottery skills to the building process. In around 3000 BCE, they began firing bricks in kilns. Kilns are ovens that reach incredibly high temperatures. Creating bricks this way was a labor- and fuel-intensive process. For that reason, the Mesopotamians saved the kiln-fired bricks for areas and buildings that would have a lot of wear, rather than for use in everyday houses. The fired bricks proved to be incredibly strong—evidence of these long-lasting building materials still exists in the area that was once Mesopotamia.

The Su Nuraxi di Barumini fort was built during the Bronze Age in Sardinia, Italy.

ENGINEERING EVOLUTIONS

Discover how masonry engineering has evolved from ancient times to today in chapter 5.

King Djoser's Step Pyramid

Made and Moved

In earlier structures, clay was molded onsite by hand to make walls. However, in the world's early cities, when clay was used to make bricks, these prefabricated units could be moved and used to build many different structures. This created a system of efficient building that had not existed before. Because the bricks were rectangular-shaped, buildings became rectangular too. This type of brick construction is still used in certain areas of the world, such as Asia, Africa, Latin America, and the Middle East.

Let's Make a Pyramid!

In around 2630 BCE, the ancient Egyptians began building the pyramids that still stand in Egypt today. An architect named Imhotep built the Step Pyramid for King Djoser. But instead of using the mud brick that had become common, the pyramid was built using six stepped layers of stone. The Step Pyramid was 204 feet (62 m) high and was the tallest building at the time.

Learning from Failure

Not long after Imhotep built the Step Pyramid for King Djoser, the first smooth pyramid was built. Known as the Red Pyramid, this was Pharaoh Sneferu's third attempt at a pyramid. His first two attempts suffered from structural problems due to their angles of incline, which made them unstable. But Sneferu learned from his mistakes and ultimately achieved success with his Red Pyramid.

A Wonder of the World

The Great Pyramid of Giza was built in around 2600 BCE. In total, three pyramids were built at Giza, with the Great Pyramid being the largest. It stood 481 feet (146 m) tall and is the only one of the original Seven Wonders of the Ancient World that is still standing. It was also the tallest building in the world for nearly 4,000 years until modern skyscrapers were constructed.

HOW IT WORKS:

TRANSPORTING MATERIALS

The Egyptians used mud bricks for the common buildings in their communities. However, they wanted something stronger and more long-lasting for their pyramids, so they used cut stone. Stone was not always available near the building sites, so the quarried stone had to be transported there. Although wheeled vehicles had been invented, the technology had not yet reached Egypt, so the Egyptians had to be creative:

Levers and sledges: They used levers and wooden sledges to transport the massive stone blocks. The huge blocks often weighed 2–15 tons (1,800–13,600 kg).

Ramps and pulling systems: They also had no way to lift the massive stones once they had transported them to the building site. To overcome this problem, the ancient Egyptians built ramps out of mud bricks and then dragged the stone blocks with ropes, to move them into place.

The design of the pyramid was a major breakthrough because it introduced incredible stability. A wide base that gradually narrows to a peak makes the structure stable and very difficult to topple.

How Did They Lift It?

The ancient Greeks and some eastern Mediterranean peoples used stone-frame building like the Egyptians, but they did not build pyramids. By around 650 BCE, the Greeks were building stone-frame structures to create large buildings. It is believed that they did so by using lifting machinery to help them place the heavy stones. There is evidence that a rope system was used to lift the stones and place them in position onsite.

Amazing Mortar

Mortar has been used for thousands of years in building. It is a paste-type substance that is used between building blocks to bond them together. Mortar hardens as it dries. It was first made out of mud and clay, and used as early as 6500 BCE in the area that is now called Pakistan. Mortar could be made from many substances, such as sand and lime.

The Greeks created early forms of cranes and levers to help them lift and position the heavy stones used for their early buildings. Today, parts of the ancient temple below are still standing in Athens, Greece.

HOW IT WORKS: LIFTING THE STONES

The ancient Greeks used an early form of crane! The heavy stones used to build some of their earliest structures had grooves cut into them. Ropes were placed along the grooves, and wrapped around the blocks. A lifting device that looked much like the modern crane was attached to the ropes. It then pulled up the stones and placed them in position. At times, the ancient Greeks also used levers to more precisely position the heavy stones.

A Concrete Idea

In the second century BCE, the Romans developed a new type of mortar that was incredibly strong. It was a pozzolanic mortar. It was named for the volcanic ash that was the secret ingredient in the strong mixture: pozzolanic ash. The Romans discovered that when they mixed pozzolanic ash with lime and water it created cement. They added it to stones and broken pieces of masonry to form concrete. They then began to build wooden molds into which they poured the concrete. The concrete then hardened into the shape they desired.

New Shapes and Structures

The discovery of concrete and using wooden forms to build molds (called frames) for buildings led to an ability to construct buildings with curved walls and structures. Though the process has evolved over time, using frames is still the basic process for creating building foundations.

BIG Breakthroughs

An important evolution in building engineering at this time was the use of fired clay roof tiles. Fired clay was much less permeable to water than the thatch roofs that had been used until this point. This meant that builders did not have to create such steeply pitched roofs to ensure the water ran off roofs.

ENGINEERING EVOLUTIONS

Discover how concrete engineering is evolving today in chapter 3. →

A Timber Comeback

While some ancient people experimented and used new building materials, the Romans discovered the usefulness of timber as a material to build trusses. Trusses are the support structures often used for roofs. They are triangular in shape and can still be seen in the framing of roofs for houses today, as well as on some bridges. The Romans did not use just timber for trusses. They also used metals, such as bronze. Metal is generally waterproof, and bronze is durable. So too is lead, which the Romans used for roofing. The use of lead allowed the Romans to set roofs at a lesser pitch because the metal is quite waterproof.

A New Iron Age

The centuries that followed the Romans saw many different types of building. Civilizations around the world used varying methods of timber, masonry, and metal construction. These methods had developed over time, but were all similar to those used by early civilizations. The greatest change in building methods came with the Industrial Revolution. This period of huge change began in Great Britain and then spread to Europe and the United States, from around 1760 to 1840. It was a time of great innovation, resulting in the development of materials such as iron.

Iron had been used in building as far back as the early Ming dynasty in China, which began in 1368. But large-scale production of iron only began in the early 1700s. By the late 1700s, new tools allowed the production of wrought-iron bars and angles, which were used as building materials. The first large cast-iron structure was a bridge over the Severn River in the United Kingdom (UK), which was completed in 1779. It is called the Iron Bridge.

Today, timber is still widely used for roof trusses.

Iron bars are placed inside concrete molds so that the concrete hardens around the bars. This provides reinforcement for the concrete, making it stronger.

What's Great about Iron?

Iron proved a useful building material because it worked well in buildings with a lot of glass. Glass allows a lot of light into buildings, which is desirable, but it is not strong enough to hold up an entire building. Iron, however, is very strong, so builders would create an iron framework and then use glass to make the building attractive and light. Iron was also easy to keep clean, so it was used in buildings such as the Hungerford Fish Market in London, UK, which was built in 1835. Timber is absorbent and so can hold moisture and bacteria. That can cause problems with mold and other sanitation issues. But iron is not absorbent, which meant it could be used for drainage too.

In the UK and other parts of northern Europe, iron also proved a reliable framing material for glass greenhouses. In these structures, a variety of plants are grown that cannot survive in the cold, damp climates of northern areas.

BIG Breakthroughs

Around the same time that the bridge over the Severn River was constructed, builders began to use iron in roof trusses and frames. Iron was not flammable, and engineers hoped this would make buildings less fire-prone. Given that fire was the heat source for buildings at this time, it was a wise idea.

Brand-New Bricks

Bricks had been used for thousands of years but they were generally mud bricks that were molded by hand. During the Industrial Revolution, a mechanical way to make bricks was created. Steel molds were created so that bricks would be a more uniform size. Hydraulic presses ensured that the building material was packed tightly into the mold, creating a very strong brick. This was combined with the use of the tunnel kiln, which is a kiln in which materials move through on a conveyer belt. This meant that bricks of consistent sizes could be mass-produced.

One of the earliest metal structures of the 1800s was the Eiffel Tower, which was completed in 1889 in Paris, France. While constructed from iron (not steel), it displayed the new, growing confidence in metal for building.

The Second Industrial Age

The second Industrial Age began in the late 1800s and saw the mass production of steel. Steel is an alloy that combines iron, carbon, and sometimes, other elements. It is extremely strong—more so than iron, which can be brittle. Steel played a major role in the development of high-rise buildings and skyscrapers because it is strong and durable. That made it a perfect frame for the gigantic skyscraping buildings created from it.

ENGINEERING EVOLUTIONS

Learn how steel engineering has evolved from the 1800s to today in chapter 4. →

Downtown Chicago has many skyscrapers. But it also has soft clay soil that required engineers to find a creative solution for the building footings.

Lessons to Learn

Builders learned a lesson with early high-rise buildings. They were heavy and depending on what they were built on, not always stable. Chicago was the site of many tall buildings, but the city lies on soft clay soil that could not support the weight of early tall buildings. Structural engineers soon realized that the spread footings the ancient Egyptians had developed would not work for such heavy buildings. Instead they used heavy timber posts and sunk them all the way down into bedrock.

BIG Breakthroughs

With steel being used for frames, builders returned to the idea of using concrete as a major building material. However, they needed something even stronger than the cement that the Romans had used to make their concrete. In 1824, Joseph Aspdin (1778–1855) patented the first artificial cement. It was stronger than the cement created by the Romans because it used clay as part of the mixture. The Romans used limestone to create their cement but clay forms stronger bonds than limestone when water is added to it. Aspdin's Portland Cement was so successful that it is still used today.

The Amazon Rain Forest has been heavily used for logging timber. In 2021, it was said that 18 trees were cut down each second within this important forest area.

Twenty-First Century Evolutions

Today, with worries about global climate change and the way human activity is affecting our environment, construction engineers have more responsibility than ever to design and build sustainably. And the materials used to construct buildings are a major environmental concern.

Many building materials use vast amounts of our precious natural resources. Timber is a great example. All buildings use wood to some extent (some more than others), and there is a finite number of trees and areas of forest. The wood supply will eventually run out. Not only is that a problem but so too is the impact that changing our forests has. Trees convert carbon dioxide to oxygen, so when we cut them down, we remove these vital natural gas converters from our environment.

Not an Endless Supply

Any building that is constructed requires sand, and sand happens to be the third most-used resource on the planet, trailing behind only air and water. Sand is a main part of cement, which is used to make concrete. It is a very commonly used construction material. While sand appears to be in great supply as a natural resource, it is finite, and not all types of sand can be used for construction. Only certain types that usually come from riverbeds, lakes, and coastlines can be used for building.

Other Modern Problems

Another environmental impact of building is the amount of waste and pollution created in the building process, and the construction industry is a big contributor to air and water pollution, as well as to landfill waste. Cement, for example, accounts for 8 percent of carbon dioxide emissions. These emissions are a major contributor to the greenhouse gases that factor in global climate change. Bricks are building materials used in many regions. The manufacturing of bricks is also very resource- and energy-intensive. Engineers are using principles of sustainable design to try to lessen the waste and pollution impacts of the building process and to preserve natural resources.

Twenty-First Century Solutions

Today, engineers are focused on safe, sustainable building practices. These allow a lot of buildings to be created with as little negative impact on our planet as possible. For example, many builders try to have pieces of buildings manufactured offsite and transferred to the jobsite. This limits the construction traffic to the jobsite, which reduces the emissions associated with construction-type vehicles. You still need the truck to bring in the pieces but you do not need all the vehicles that would be associated with building the components onsite.

The timber industry is also working to use sustainable forestry practices where possible, including planting new trees when mature trees are cut down. In working sustainably, engineers are using many of the same basic building techniques used in long-ago times. However, the building processes and techniques are evolving to meet the demands of our changing times.

The Line is an exciting sustainable, futuristic city project in the Saudi Arabian desert. It aims to use renewable energy sources and to create an eco-friendly space. Could this be the future of all modern construction?

CHAPTER 2

A TIMBER EVOLUTION

The timber industry is working on sustainable practices that will ensure our forests are not destroyed.

The use of timber has gone in and out of fashion over the thousands of years since nomadic people used it to build their tentlike structures. The movement away from timber in some types of construction has been the result of builders looking for materials that are stronger or more long-lasting, as well as fireproof. But today, engineers are returning to using timber. That is in part because it is a more sustainable resource than some other building materials. It is also because builders are finding ways to increase the durability of timber.

Timber and Lumber

Timber refers to trees or tree wood that has not yet been cut or processed. Lumber, on the other hand, refers to wood that has been processed to make beams, planks, and boards. So when we talk about using timber as a building material, it needs to first be processed into lumber.

Lumber is used to build new homes, like this one.

HOW IT WORKS:
MAKING LUMBER

Timber becomes lumber in the following process:

1. A tree is cut down in the forest and transported to the sawmill.
2. The tree is roughly cut into boards, beams, or other pieces.
3. Irregular edges and defects are removed from these cut pieces.
4. The edges of the cut pieces are further trimmed so that the resulting pieces are all a uniform size.
5. Pieces are sorted based on their size and what they will be used for. Some pieces are left "green." Some uses for lumber require wood that is not processed through a kiln. However, most wood is dried in the kiln, because the final product is stronger than that of green wood.
6. The wood that is intended to be dried and processed is put in the kiln, which dries the wood. The kiln can be run at different temperatures and levels of humidity based on how much moisture content is to be removed from the wood.
7. After the kiln-drying process, the wood is planed to ensure a smooth surface and a consistent thickness.

ENGINEERING SOLUTIONS

Trees are some of our most precious natural resources. And we have heard about the dangers of cutting down forests. So it may surprise you to learn that timber is considered a sustainable resource. It is true: Trees do a lot for our environment and we need to make sure we do not deforest our planet. However, engineers have developed sustainable practices for using wood that do make it an environmentally conscious choice. These include selective logging rather then clear-cutting huge areas of forest, reforesting areas where trees have been harvested, and using environmentally friendly logging equipment and machinery.

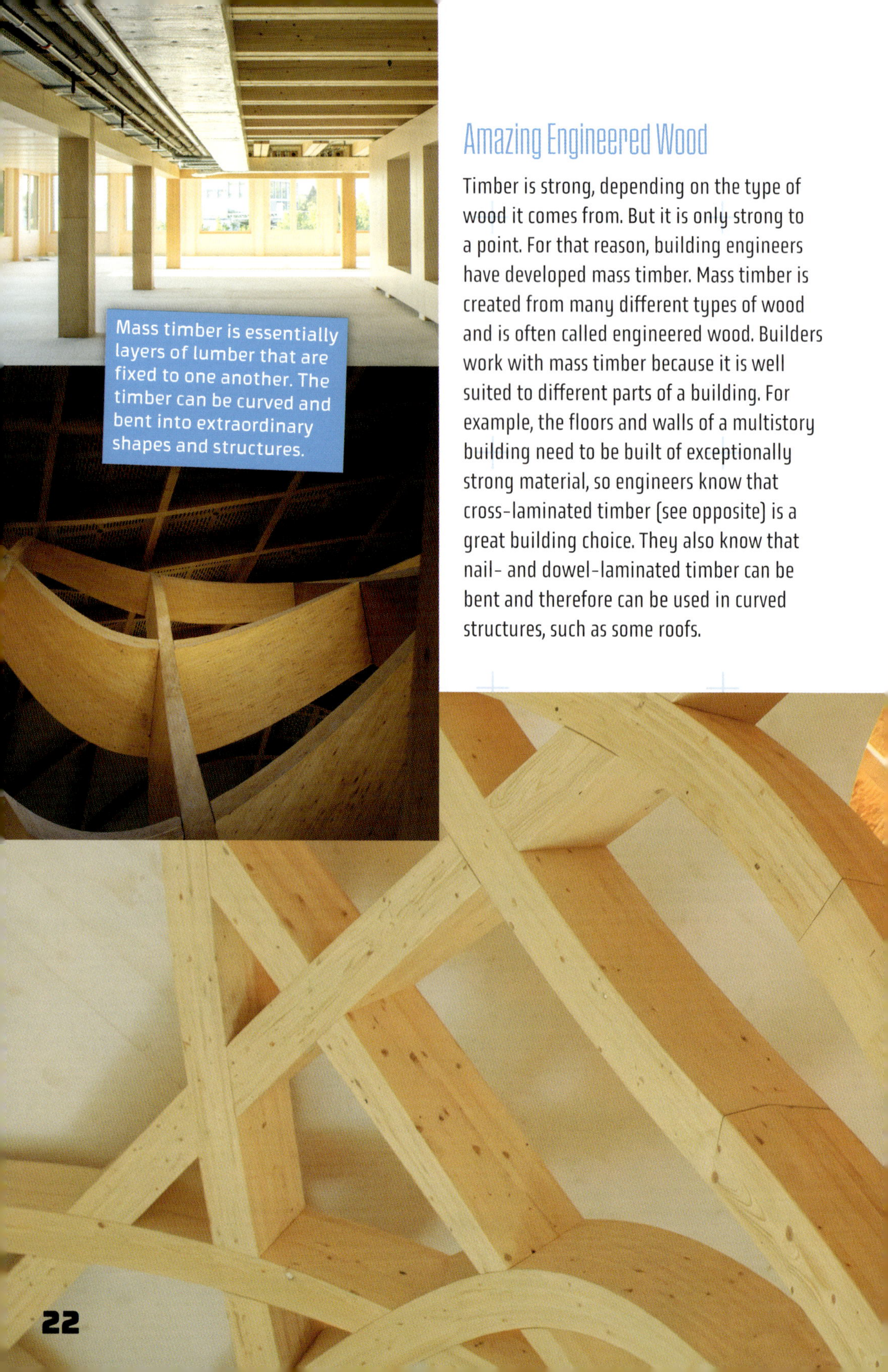

Mass timber is essentially layers of lumber that are fixed to one another. The timber can be curved and bent into extraordinary shapes and structures.

Amazing Engineered Wood

Timber is strong, depending on the type of wood it comes from. But it is only strong to a point. For that reason, building engineers have developed mass timber. Mass timber is created from many different types of wood and is often called engineered wood. Builders work with mass timber because it is well suited to different parts of a building. For example, the floors and walls of a multistory building need to be built of exceptionally strong material, so engineers know that cross-laminated timber (see opposite) is a great building choice. They also know that nail- and dowel-laminated timber can be bent and therefore can be used in curved structures, such as some roofs.

HOW IT WORKS:

MAKING MASS TIMBER

There are a number of types of mass timber:

- **Cross-laminated timber:** To create this type of mass timber, lumber is dried in a kiln and is then stacked and glued in layers at 90-degree angles. There are usually three to nine layers of lumber in total. Imagine a square piece of wood. Then imagine taking another square piece of wood the same size, rotating it 90 degrees, and gluing it on top of the first layer. And then doing that several more times with same-size squares of wood. When you finish, you would have a stack of glued-together panels of wood that would be extremely durable. Because it is extremely strong, cross-laminated timber can be used in parts of buildings that need to withstand great amounts of weight.
- **Nail-laminated timber:** To create this type of mass timber, strips of lumber are stacked together on their edges and then fastened with nails or screws.
- **Dowel-laminated timber:** The process to create this type of mass timber is like nail lamination, except wooden dowels are used in place of metal nails or screws.
- **Laminated-strand lumber:** This type of mass timber takes dried strands or flakes of wood and packs them together. Moisture-resistant adhesive is used to bond them. This process is a little like sweeping up bits of wood scraps from a project and molding them into a block. You fix the scraps together with adhesive.
- **Parallel-strand lumber:** This type of mass timber is created in the same way as laminated-strand lumber. However, the strands of lumber tend to be longer and are laid parallel, which may not be the case for laminated-strand lumber. Think of those same wood scraps swept up from a project. However, you would take more care in molding them into the form you want, making sure the strands were parallel. This is generally done because it creates a striking, finished texture on the wood.

Reducing Our Carbon Footprint

You have probably heard about the importance of reducing our carbon footprint. That is the amount of greenhouse gas emissions (including carbon dioxide and methane) we generate. Carbon dioxide is a greenhouse gas, and trees help the environment by absorbing and storing carbon dioxide so it is not released into the atmosphere. When it comes to building, this is an important consideration. That is because carbon dioxide remains stored even when a tree is cut down and processed into lumber or mass timber. Of course, if the tree is not cut down, the same would be true: The tree would continue storing the carbon dioxide. The difference is that the process of constructing buildings from concrete and steel *gives off* carbon dioxide. However, constructing a building from timber *stores* carbon dioxide.

Timber to the Rescue

The Environmental and Energy Study Institute (EESI) has made some important findings. It has discovered that using mass timber instead of concrete or steel in building can make a big difference to greenhouse gas emissions. It reduces greenhouse gas emissions from the building process between 13 and 26.5 percent. And the World Economic Forum (WEF) states that a traditional concrete and steel building produces around 1,968 tons (2,000 mt) of carbon dioxide emissions. Reducing that very large number by 13 to 26.5 percent is a huge help to the environment.

Today, the construction industry is focussing on reducing harmful emissions that affect Earth's delicate atmosphere.

ENGINEERING SOLUTIONS

The more vehicles that are at a construction site, the greater the environmental impact is. Vehicles produce greenhouse gas emissions and increase traffic. They also result in wear and tear on roadways, which then need repairs. This has led building engineers to use prefabricated materials whenever possible. Timber is ideally suited for this because it is fairly light and easy to transport. So features such as roof trusses, window casings, and support beams can be made offsite and then transported to a building site.

BIG Breakthroughs

Sweden is a country well known for its work on environmental sustainability. There, engineers have built the 20-story Sara Cultural Centre almost entirely out of timber. The building has a library, banquet halls, three theaters, and a hotel. It also has a restaurant, exhibit spaces, and a rooftop pool and spa. The pieces of the building were prefabricated offsite, so reducing the number of vehicles needed at the construction site. Reducing the amount of transportation needed in building is also a sustainable practice.

Not only is it a sturdy building, it is also carbon negative. That means it takes in or holds more carbon dioxide than was created by building it. The building process gave off 5,631 tons (5,108 mt) of carbon dioxide. However, the amount of carbon dioxide contained in the timber is 9,095 tons (8,251 mt). If the building had been made of concrete or steel, the building process would have given off carbon dioxide but none would have been retained.

The Sara Cultural Centre in Sweden is a great example of sustainable building.

Building to Help Earth

More and more engineers are recognizing how using timber as a building material can really help our planet. So, they are trying to use the material as much as possible. Traditional timber was not strong enough to use for larger structures. However, mass timber has made building skyscrapers out of wood products a very real possibility. For example, in Milwaukee, Wisconsin, the Ascent luxury apartment and retail building soars 25 stories above the ground. And it is made of timber.

Fire Escape?

Wood is highly flammable. For that reason, mass timber products are treated with a fire-retardant coating. With the coating, if they catch alight, they slowly char rather than quickly going up in flames. They burn at a slower and steadier rate than other materials such as steel. The way the timber burns is also more predictable. For example, steel can melt and then suddenly fold during a fire.

Responsible Forestry

While trees are very important to our ecosystem, forest overgrowth can lead to catastrophic wildfires. In fact, the National Forest Service (NFS) has declared that overgrown forests are a major problem in what they call a "full-blown wildfire and forest health crisis." Cutting down out-of-control forests could provide us with timber and avoid wildfires. However, certain types of trees are more useful than others in building. For that reason, it is not as simple as just logging excess trees. That is why environmental engineers have created guidelines for sustainable logging practices. These preserve the health of the forest and its inhabitants. They also enable the building industry to use the logged timber as a building material.

The Wood Hotel in Norway is a great example of a wooden skyscraper.

Using drones, a forest's health and growth can be monitored.

BIG Breakthroughs

Precision forests are now being used to sustainably produce timber for the building industry. Engineers have revolutionized forestry management by using satellites, drones, and sensors. They monitor temperature, dryness, and fire. They also monitor storm damage and overall tree health in precision forests. For each tree harvested, several seedlings are planted. Then these seedlings and the growing trees are carefully monitored to make sure the forest stays healthy. In this way, environmental engineers are working with construction engineers to create many more sustainable building practices and materials.

Lightweight but Strong

Timber is lighter than steel or concrete. This has interested building engineers because using timber allows for the creation of a shallow foundation. Shallow foundations typically spread out the load of a building, keeping it close to the surface of the earth. Whereas deep foundations require the builder to excavate much farther down. They also require piles or piers to support the building. Shallow foundations are both cost-effective and typically more environmentally friendly. That has led building engineers to use timber for building when they can. As the building industry continues to look toward more sustainable building practices, it is likely that timber will play a big role in future construction projects.

CHAPTER 3

A CONCRETE EVOLUTION

Concrete is a building material that is made by adding aggregate—gravel, sand, and other materials—to cement. Cement is the binder that holds together the aggregate. The cement mixture then hardens into concrete.

How Do We Use Concrete?

Concrete is used in many building applications. It is used for driveways and walkways, for example, but it is also used for buildings. All buildings have a foundation made of concrete. The foundation makes sure the building is structurally solid. Some buildings are constructed using concrete blocks.

Cons of Concrete

One problem with concrete is that it leaves a big carbon footprint. That is because a lot of energy is needed to create it, and doing so creates carbon dioxide emissions. However, despite the environmental impacts of using concrete, there are still many situations in which using concrete is the best choice for building.

Concrete can be used to make amazing structures. It is also a practical material to use for walkways.

HOW IT WORKS:
CREATING CONCRETE

Concrete is made by mixing cement with water and aggregates in the following process:

1. **Make cement:** Calcium silicates and sulfate are ground into a fine powder. The powder is then heated and burned to become a material known as clinker. The clinker is then ground until it is a fine powder.
2. **Proportion the concrete:** Concrete is made of cement (usually Portland), water, and aggregates, such as gravel, crushed stone, or sand. How those elements are proportioned depends on how and where the concrete will be used. Different proportions of various types of aggregate will change the weight and strength of concrete. They will also affect how long-lasting it is and how much moisture it contains.
3. **Mix the concrete:** In this process, the elements are mixed together.
4. **Hydrate the mixture:** When water is added to the mixture, it creates a chemical reaction called hydration. The cement gets stronger and coats the pieces of aggregate in the mixture.
5. **Place the concrete:** After the hydration process has completed, the concrete needs to be placed before it begins to harden. Hoppers, chutes, and buckets are all tools used in this part of the process. How the concrete is placed depends on where and how it will be used. Concrete foundations are often poured with the use of a concrete boom pump. This looks like a truck with a giant arm that acts as a long tunnel through which the concrete flows. Builders aim the end of the arm into the foundation where the concrete needs to be poured. Concrete blocks, on the other hand, are made in molds.
6. **Cure the concrete:** The curing process depends on the type of concrete and the weather. In general, the process involves keeping the concrete moistened while it hardens and gains strength.

Concrete Comeback

Like timber, concrete went through a period of not often being used. However, as the demand for bigger and taller buildings grew, so too did the demand for stronger materials to make them. Wood does not have great tensile strength. Tensile strength is the stress that a building material can support without breaking. So the search was on to find a tougher material, and builders turned once more to concrete for construction.

Concrete is poured over reinforcing bars to create the floor of a building.

Adding Iron for Strength

In the 1860s, Joseph Monier (1823–1906) found that if he embedded iron mesh in a concrete mold, it had much greater tensile strength. This became known as reinforced concrete. Since then, reinforced concrete has evolved to a point at which it is strong enough to be used in very large buildings that bear a lot of weight.

Made Even Tougher

While nonreinforced concrete does not have a great tensile strength, it has good compressive strength. This is the amount of weight a material can bear without being crushed. Today rebar, which is an abbreviation for reinforcing bar, is often used to reinforce concrete and create more tensile strength. Reinforcing bars are thin, very strong bars of metal that can be put inside concrete to make it stronger. That way, if the concrete crumbles, the rebar is still inside to preserve the strength.

ENGINEERING SOLUTIONS

One problem building engineers have faced when using concrete is cracking. Concrete can crack when the earth under it moves. The resulting cracks are called settlement cracks. Concrete can also crack as it shrinks, expands, or flexes. It does so as a result of weather conditions or if the concrete has not been properly cured or mixed. It can also happen when the reinforcement inside the concrete corrodes. However, engineers have discovered ways to make self-healing concrete! This is concrete that can repair its own cracks. There are a number of ways to make self-healing concrete. One of the most promising is bioengineering. In this process bacteria is used within the concrete to "heal" the cracks (see page 47).

BIG Breakthroughs

Another exciting development is translucent concrete. Engineers have discovered that putting optical fibers into the concrete mixture allows light to pass through the mixture. Natural light makes spaces look brighter and more appealing. Windows in buildings bring in outside light, and translucent concrete allows even more outside light.

As well as looking great, there is also another benefit to bringing in more natural light. Artificial lighting draws electricity from the power grid, which is bad for the environment. The more natural light we can bring into a building, the less artificial light needs to be used. So concrete that allows light to pass through is an exciting new breakthrough in construction.

One of the tallest buildings in the world, the Burj Khalifa in Dubai, was built using 11.6 million cubic feet (330,000 cubic m) of concrete.

Concrete and the Environment

A major concern with using concrete as a building material has been its impact on the environment. The creation of concrete itself does not produce carbon emissions. However, the creation of cement does, and cement is a necessary part of concrete.

To create cement, limestone, clay, and other materials are fired in a kiln. The energy used to power the kiln produces carbon dioxide. So too does the chemical reaction that is produced by the firing process. For each pound (0.45 kg) of concrete produced, the National Ready Mixed Concrete Association (NRMCA) says that 0.93 pounds (0.4 kg) of carbon dioxide is produced. This is not an insignificant amount. Overall, it is thought that the cement industry produces 4 billion tons (3.6 mt) of carbon per year.

Depending on the amount of cement needed, it is often still mixed by hand or using a small cement mixer. Larger amounts of cement such as those needed on a construction site are mixed by a heavy-duty cement mixer.

Waste Not, Want Not

When old buildings are knocked down, they leave behind a lot of concrete, and especially the heavy pieces used in the foundations. Instead of throwing that concrete away, engineers have found ways to recycle it. Large chunks of old concrete can be broken into smaller pieces and used again. These pieces, called aggregate, can be mixed into new concrete.

Recycled concrete can also be crushed into sand. This sand is great for building the base layer of a road or for making the foundation of a new building. Using old concrete saves natural resources like gravel and river sand, which take a long time to form in nature. It also keeps construction waste out of landfills and helps protect the environment. Sustainable practices like this one will become increasingly important as more cities grow. Recycling concrete will help reduce the amount of new materials that need to be mined and transported.

There's a Downside

The downside to recycling is that the concrete does not look very attractive. Often the aggregate used in concrete for things that will be seen by people is small stones or another attractive material. Broken-down concrete does not look as pretty as small stones. However, there are uses of concrete that are not seen, and recycled concrete works well for construction projects that are hidden.

ENGINEERING SOLUTIONS

To combat the problems with carbon emissions, engineers are coming up with smart ways to reuse carbon dioxide waste. One company called ThalesNano Energy converts carbon dioxide waste into fuels or chemical feedstocks. These are the raw materials that are used in the mass production of chemical products. One popular idea is that the cement industry could partner with such a company to reuse the carbon dioxide waste in a productive way.

There are also green cement technologies used by companies such as Solida. The carbon emissions produced by the kiln are added to the open spaces in the cement. The cement is then cured with carbon dioxide, rather than water. That speeds up the curing process and creates a stronger product. Overall, this green cement process may reduce carbon emissions by about 30 percent. That is a sizeable reduction in output.

New Printing and Concrete

Three-dimensional, or 3D printing, is becoming a revolutionary tool in the building and concrete industries. Engineers have been experimenting with printing 3D houses and other structures in recent years. And they have had success. One benefit to 3D printing concrete structures is that less waste is created. Because the printers make exactly what is needed, few materials are wasted. There is also no need to use wood or other materials to build molds or forms for the concrete. That is because it is not poured as it is in traditional concrete building. The printer can also work around the clock, without needing to rest. That means it can build faster. There is also no need for a large crew to work with the concrete molds or build the structure's frame.

The Dubai Future Academy is the world's very first commercial building to be created by a 3D printer.

HOW IT WORKS: BUILDING WITH 3D PRINTING

3D printing can be used for multiple types of construction. The process is largely the same in all of them.

1. An architect or engineer uses a computer-aided design (CAD) program to create the design of the structure.
2. The information from the CAD design is sent to the 3D printer.
3. The appropriate building material (concrete, resin, plastic, or metal, for example) is loaded into the 3D printer.
4. The printer creates the structure by adding thin layers of the material until the structure is complete and ready.

3D printers can create entire structures. They can also print components that are then put together to build the structure.

When the building industry first started experimenting with 3D printing, engineers ran into a problem. Concrete is designed to harden, and that can happen in the printing process. When it happens, the concrete can clog the nozzle of the printer. The engineers at Mexican cement company CEMEX and 3D construction-printing company COBOD found a way around this issue. They created a product called D.fab. D.fab can be added to a traditional concrete mix to make it flow more smoothly. That allows it to be used effectively in 3D printers.

Good for the Planet

The environmental impact of 3D printing concrete structures is also big. For one, the printing is done onsite. That means fewer trucks traveling to and from the jobsite, which lowers carbon emissions from vehicle traffic. Local materials, such as sands and soils, can often be used in the concrete mixture. That reduces the need to bring in materials from other areas. Someday, we may even be able to build structures on the moon or Mars using 3D printing. We would do so by using the soil there in a concrete mixture that can be printed into buildings. The National Aeronautics and Space Administration (NASA) has a goal to do just that on the moon by 2040. That will be a giant step forward for the construction industry.

Architects work on plans for a building, which are then fed to the 3D printer for the construction phase.

Printing a building

CHAPTER 4

A STEEL EVOLUTION

Steel is produced in a foundry under extreme heat.

It is believed that steel may have been around since as early as 1800 BCE. Modern steel-production techniques have been around since the seventeenth century. Steel is incredibly strong and durable. It also has a very high tensile strength. For those reasons, building engineers have long used it to construct skyscrapers and bridges. Steel is also versatile and can be used in different ways.

Problems with Steel

One drawback to using steel as a building material is that it rusts or corrodes. That has stopped engineers using the material in places where rust or corrosion might be more likely, for example near the ocean or in very humid climates. Corrosion can cause steel to break or buckle, making buildings unstable. However, new coatings and paints that contain zinc are a good solution to this problem. They slow the damage caused by rust or corrosion and that makes the steel last a lot longer.

Steel helps architects and construction workers create stunning buildings. However, steel rebar can corrode and rust, which weakens its structural integrity.

HOW IT WORKS:
CREATING STEEL

The raw materials for steel come from iron ore. This is found naturally in iron, oxygen, and other minerals. It also includes carbon, which is found in coal. This is how steel is made:

1. **Iron ore and coal are mined:** Iron and coal can be mined in open-pit mines or in underground mines.
2. **Coal becomes coke:** The coal is heated in an oven without oxygen to a very high temperature—more than 2,000 degrees Fahrenheit (1,093 °C). That heat gets rid of unstable materials in the coal. What is left is a hard, porous substance called coke.
3. **Raw materials are turned into liquid iron:** Iron ore is combined with limestone and the coke. It is then put in a blast furnace. There, the mixture melts and becomes molten iron.
4. **Molten iron is turned into raw steel:** There are two ways this can happen. Using an electric arc furnace, raw steel is created when electricity is forced through the furnace. This purifies, or removes unwanted parts, from the iron. The second method is using an oxygen furnace. Scrap steel is pushed into the molten iron. The mixture is then forced through the furnace, which purifies the iron. Both methods result in raw steel.
5. **The raw steel is refined:** When the liquid iron is turned into raw steel, certain unwanted elements remain in the substance. Steel industry workers use different methods to improve the steel until it is suitable for use.
6. **The raw steel is cast:** After the raw steel is refined, it is cast into molds. It then cools. As the steel cools, it is malleable. That means it can be formed into different shapes. These can include beams, wires, flat sheets, or strips.
7. **The steel is formed:** Steel industry workers use hot rollers to further form the cast steel. Then, steelmakers shape the steel product into whatever is needed for the building.

Prefabricated components for building are becoming increasingly popular in modular house designs.

Made in Advance

As with timber, prefabrication of steel building components is a real timesaver. Steel mills can create the exact pieces needed for a building based on specifications provided by engineers and architects. The pieces are then transported to the jobsite. This has also limited the amount of waste created in the construction process. When the pieces are created to the exact specifications, there is no waste—a win for the environment.

What about Waste?

But what if there is waste? What if a builder orders too much of some steel products? Steel is completely recyclable, so waste and scraps are collected and then taken to a recycling center. The waste is processed and then sent to a mill or foundry. There, the steel scraps are melted down, purified, and cast into sheets. Because steel is recyclable, it also means that when a building using steel components is demolished, the steel can be recycled and then reused.

ENGINEERING SOLUTIONS

One issue with steel recycling is that steel scrap material often contains other metals, such as copper. This can cause cracks in steel during processing. That weakens the steel as a result. However, engineers at the University of Toronto in Canada have developed a new steel recycling method. It involves using an electrochemical process to remove copper and carbon impurities from recycled steel once it is heated and turned into molten steel.

Super Steel

Engineers have been trying to create a stronger, more durable "super steel" for a long time. Decades ago, Russian engineers added aluminum to steel. That created a very strong, lightweight steel alloy. However, it was also quite brittle. It turned out that crystals created when the aluminum and iron atoms fused were causing the cracking problem.

Decades later, South Korean scientists developed a method to separate the crystals from one another. That prevented them from splintering. They added a bit of nickel, too. It gave them more control over the formation of the crystals. However, the crystals still existed, and the steel was still a little brittle. The South Korean engineers then tried adding titanium atoms to the alloy. Titanium is incredibly strong, and there is also plenty of it. Titanium prevented the crystals from forming and fixed the problem. However, titanium is very expensive and is also difficult to process, so it is not perfect.

Still Seeking Solutions

Some recent promise has been shown when manganese is added to a steel alloy. However, there are concerns about the availability of manganese, which has to be mined from Earth's crust. And the mining of manganese can harm both the environment and the health of miners. So engineers are still on a mission to create a super steel.

While wood is often used for roof trusses, steel can be used, too.

Flexibility Is Key

Flexibility is a building's ability to move. That is crucial in areas that have a lot of movement from seismic activity, such as earthquakes, or that experience high winds. When engineers design structures for these areas, they design them with flexibility in mind. They want the building to move with the earth, not stand rigid and crumble when the earth begins to shake or the wind is really strong. However, masonry is not flexible, so in areas where flexibility is important, builders tend to use steel instead.

ENGINEERING SOLUTIONS

Several companies have begun making more flexible steel so that buildings in areas with a lot of seismic activity are even safer. Taylor Devices, for example, has created fluid viscous dampers (FVDs) to do just that. These devices absorb the movement that occurs in a structure from earthquakes or high winds. They capture the energy of movement and convert it to heat energy. This heat energy is then safely released into the air.

Tokyo, Japan (shown below), is prone to earthquakes. Some buildings, like this one shown left, are reinforced with steel braces to prevent them from collapsing during an earthquake.

Steel is joined by welding. However, the welded joints are not as strong as the steel itself.

Strength Solutions

Another issue with steel can be its decreased strength at welded joints. Welding is a process where metal parts are joined by heating their surfaces to the melting point and then pressing or hammering them together before they cool. What results is a larger steel component with a joint where the independent pieces are melted together. That joint can be less strong than the steel and can be a point of weakness.

Some companies are working on solutions that minimize the need for welding. For example, Atlas Tube and another company called Nippon Steel Engineering worked together to create large hollow tubes of steel that can be used as support columns. These hollow tubes can carry a heavy load in terms of structure and because they are quite large, fewer pieces must be welded together. This means that there are fewer weld joints and structural vulnerabilities.

Fireproofing a Building

Buildings need to be protected from fire. If there is a fire, the steel becomes weaker and can cause a building to suffer structural damage. While the whole building may not collapse, sections of it can. To prevent this from happening, any steel that is used as part of a frame or as a support needs to be fire resistant. A company called Black Rock creates steel support columns, but these supports contain insulating material and a concrete core. Both make them more fireproof.

Building a Sustainable Future

As with using other building materials, using steel for construction has a big impact on the environment. Engineers are continuing to develop environmentally friendly production processes for steel. For example, producing steel requires a lot of energy, so some steel production companies are using renewable energy sources, such as solar, wind, and hydro power, to complete the production process, rather than just relying on fossil fuels for energy.

Companies are also recycling steel scrap to minimize waste. Steel is completely recyclable, so in theory there should never be any wasted steel. It can always be reused. The steel production process also produces a lot of carbon dioxide emissions. Production companies are trying to capture and store the carbon dioxide produced in the production process, rather than releasing it into the environment. Steel producers are also using digital sensors to ensure the greatest efficiency in each step of the production process, further reducing unnecessary emissions.

If the construction industry can rely more on energy created by wind or solar power, it will be better for the environment.

This pedestrian bridge in Amsterdam was built using a 3D printer. It will be monitored to gauge its stability and strength

A Three-Dimensional Picture

Just as concrete can be 3D printed, so can steel. In years past, smaller metal parts and components have been 3D printed. But now, companies like FRAMECAD and LifeTec Construction Group are using CAD and 3D printing technologies to create entire steel building frames. They are then shipped to the jobsite and assembled there. While a 3D printer is not big enough to print an entire frame of a skyscraper onsite, it can create pieces of the steel building frame, which can then be assembled like a puzzle at the jobsite.

In a step forward for 3D printing, Dutch engineers 3D printed a 40-foot (12 m) steel pedestrian bridge. It spans a canal in Amsterdam, in the Netherlands. The bridge carries many pedestrians every day. It has sensors that collect data about its performance and health, so it can be a study for future similar structures.

ENGINEERING SOLUTIONS

One of the byproducts of the steel production process is slag. This is a solid waste product. Engineers have tried to find uses for slag, but it is often just thrown away. This takes up precious landfill space. Slag also contains chemicals that can be harmful to the environment if not properly treated before disposal. However, engineers in the UK have been working on a process that turns slag into cement. Given that cement is often used in the same construction projects as steel, this could be a real step forward for sustainable building projects.

CHAPTER 5

A MASONRY EVOLUTION

Masonry is thought to be among the oldest construction techniques. Masonry construction can include anything from laying tile floors and concrete-paver patios to building natural-stone fireplaces and entire brick houses. Masonry structures were built to last. The fact that tholoi ruins and the pyramids still stand today is proof of that. However, there is always room for innovation and improvement, and masonry construction has evolved with the times.

Working by Hand

The general building process still involves masons laying building materials by hand. While much masonry work is still done by hand, there has been some movement to automate it. This means machines or computers do the work rather than people. For example, some builders now use bricklaying robots such as the Semi-Automated Mason, or SAM. SAM was designed to assist human bricklayers, not replace them. It uses a conveyer system and sensors to guide placement of bricks. Human workers still do certain parts of the process, like removing excess mortar.

The Great Wall of China is a great example of masonry construction. It is the longest structure ever built at 13, 170.5 miles (21,196 km) long and 30 feet (9 m) wide.

HOW IT WORKS:
MASONRY BUILDING

The steps for building a brick masonry structure usually include the following:

1. **Spread the first layer of mortar and create a trench:** The bricklayer starts with a generous layer of mortar and trims off any excess. A trench in the mortar is then made. It is shaped to the size of the bricks that will be laid.
2. **Lay down the first layer of bricks:** Mortar is applied to the short end of each brick. That creates a joint between that brick and the next one.
3. **Level the first layer of bricks:** When the first row of bricks is laid, a level is used to make sure the bricks are level. Any that are not are repositioned.
4. **Apply mortar to the top of the first layer of bricks:** A generous amount of mortar is then spread on the top of the first layer of bricks and any excess is trimmed to keep the surface neat.
5. **Lay down the next layer of bricks:** The steps are repeated to create the next layer of bricks. However, this time around the bricks are staggered so that the vertical joints between layers of bricks are offset. This strengthens the bonds between the bricks.

Staggered Bricks

If bricks are all stacked exactly on top of one another, the joints match up on each row. That means the structure will not be strong. The joints will be more prone to shrinking and cracking. If the bricks are aligned, it is also very easy for a small crack to make its way up a wall. There are many different bond patterns that are much stronger, and they are often used when creating brick structures.

Builders use a brick trowel (shown below) and a level to make sure their work is accurate.

Mass-produced concrete blocks can be a cost-effective building solution.

From Clay to Concrete

Originally, masonry structures were built from stones and, later, from clay bricks. Clay bricks are still used today, though some bricks use other materials, such as sand lime or fly ash. Fly ash is the residue from crushed coal. This is often made when coal is burned for energy or in the making of steel. However, concrete is also a material that is often used in masonry. Concrete can be reinforced with steel, which improves its strength and durability. It is also a versatile product since a number of different materials, such as gravel, rocks, or sand, can be used as aggregate in the concrete.

Concrete can be poured into large molds, such as when pouring a building foundation. It can also be poured into smaller forms, where it hardens into blocks. Those concrete blocks can then be placed as bricks would be, to form walls. When a builder is working on something that will be a pretty simple or common design, concrete blocks can be very useful. Think of an apartment complex where every building will have the same basic design. For a project like that, concrete blocks can be a very efficient way to create the basic structure. They are a uniform size and shape and can be used to create many different structures that all have the same basic dimensions.

ENGINEERING SOLUTIONS

Waste is always a concern in building. Waste fills up landfills and can introduce toxic chemicals into the surrounding land. That is why engineers are always looking for sustainable solutions, and that means finding ways to use as much of a material as possible while leaving little waste.

Concrete is great for this. This material is made from cement and aggregate, so engineers have experimented with using recyclable materials as aggregate. It does not have to always be gravel or stones.

Recently, crushed glass and fly ash have been used in concrete mixes. Fly ash is a fine powder left over from burning coal or making steel. It can be added to concrete to improve strength and reduce waste. Crushed glass can also be used as a fine aggregate, replacing sand. These materials help reduce the need for mining new resources.

In theory, fly ash from steelmaking could be reused in concrete, and then recycled again in future projects. That would create a perfect circle of sustainability, where waste becomes a useful building material again and again.

Self-Healing Masonry

Like concrete, masonry can crack, and mortar can shrink. The natural movement of the earth can also eventually cause the hardened material to crack. To deal with this, engineers are working on developing self-healing masonry materials, and, as mentioned earlier, bacteria can help. It can be manipulated with "helper chemicals" to produce mineral deposits such as calcium carbonate. That is a main part of rocks and other masonry materials. So, when bacteria are introduced to a masonry structure, they deposit the mineral deposits and "heal" the cracks.

Masons have to use tools like this bubble level to ensure that masonry construction is as level as possible.

Masonry for Energy Efficiency

One benefit of masonry construction is that it tends to be quite energy efficient. That means it stops heat escaping from a building, and stops the building overheating too. Bricks absorb and store heat and then slowly release it into the interior of a structure, so a brick house in the beating summer sun will not heat up as fast as a house constructed of wood. That is because the bricks provide insulation. This is known as thermal mass.

ENGINEERING SOLUTIONS

Masonry-constructed buildings are naturally energy efficient because of their thermal mass. However, there is always room for improvement. When it is 100 degrees Fahrenheit (38 °C) outside, even a brick home will eventually heat up. And when it is -20 degrees Fahrenheit (-29 °C), even a brick home will be cold. Engineers have come up with several solutions to this. Some masonry walls have space in them because concrete blocks are formed with hollow centers. In these types of walls, insulation can be "blown" into the spaces in the concrete blocks. However, even if a masonry wall is solid, there are still options. Engineers have developed rigid foam boards that can be placed over the wall. Siding or drywall is then placed over the insulation to create a finished look.

Polystyrene foam can be placed over masonry construction for insulation. Insulation keeps a building warm in winter and cooler in summer.

Brick houses are very common in certain areas where seismic activity is not an issue.

An Unstable Earth

Brick houses are commonly seen in certain parts of the United States. The stately old brick homes in the East and South are a common architectural style. But brick homes are rarely seen in other areas, such as California and the Pacific Northwest. This is because masonry construction does not withstand the shifting of the earth as well as other types of construction. In areas with a lot of seismic activity, the ground is constantly shifting and settling, and cracks can easily form. Unreinforced brick structures can crumble in a powerful earthquake.

Engineering for Natural Disasters

Engineers have developed ways to reinforce older brick structures that were built before building codes required earthquake-safe building practices. Such techniques involve using structural steel connectors. They absorb the seismic waves produced by the earthquake. They then distribute them throughout the structure, so that they are not concentrated in one weak area. Shear walls can be strategically placed in a structure. They absorb the impact of the earthquake and reduce the movement of the rest of the structure. These same building techniques are used in areas prone to other natural disasters that can damage buildings, such as hurricanes or floods.

Using the Power of the Sun

Solar energy has become a major focus as scientists and engineers have sought to find renewable energy sources to reduce our reliance on fossil fuels. Traditionally, solar power has been captured through the use of solar photovoltaics, or solar panels. They are installed on the roofs of houses or buildings, or erected in solar farms. However, engineers at companies such as SolaBlock have developed solar solutions worked into masonry blocks.

Solar panels are becoming increasingly common on buildings. In the future, we may see more masonry blocks with inbuilt solar panels.

Used on the Outside

Solar blocks are currently used for building façades, not structural walls. That is because they are not capable of bearing the load of a building. In façades, they can be used in place of traditional masonry blocks. The blocks contain high-performance crystalline silicon cells. They collect solar energy in much the same way that solar photovoltaics do. SolaBlock intends to produce a structural version of the blocks in the near future, which can be used to bear the loads of buildings.

Other Sunny Fixes

Other companies, such as Solar Masonry, have come up with smart solutions too. They have incorporated solar photovoltaic panels on the sides of masonry blocks to capture the sun's energy. It is then converted into usable electricity. The blocks serve the same function as those created by companies like SolaBlock. However, they have a clearly visible solar photovoltaic panel on the side of each unit, which some consider less attractive.

Smart with Sensors

Engineers are also developing ways to use smart bricks that are embedded with sensors to monitor the health of a building. The data collected can include structural data, such as where cracks are occurring. It can also include data about the temperature, humidity, or air inside a building. This data can be used to maintain the structural integrity of the building or to heat and cool the building efficiently. That's smart engineering!

ENGINEERING SOLUTIONS

Along similar lines as solar blocks, scientists have developed a way to turn ordinary bricks into energy-storage devices. They created a PEDOT coating that can be painted on bricks to turn them into energy-storage sponges. PEDOT is a polymer made of nanofibers that can conduct electricity. When painted onto fired bricks, it is absorbed into the bricks, which are porous. The iron oxide in red bricks triggers a polymerization reaction. That then allows the bricks to soak up energy, most likely from solar cells. The bricks serve as supercapacitors, which can store and deliver energy. They work like high-powered, rechargeable batteries.

BIG Breakthroughs

Researchers are working to develop "living bricks." These are special building blocks that can help make buildings more sustainable. The bricks can turn liquid waste into clean water. They also use microbial fuel cells to create bioelectricity, which can help power lights or small devices in a building.

The microbial fuel cells work by using sunlight, air, and liquid waste. Inside the brick, tiny microbes feed on the waste. Through chemical reactions, they produce electrons, which create electricity. And for added value, at the same time, the waste is cleaned and turned into water that can be reused.

Constructing Consciously

Water conservation is a current focus for environmentally conscious builders and homeowners. That is especially true in dry places, such as California and Arizona. California is perpetually in a state of drought. Even during rainy years, conserving water is at the top of people's minds. Rainwater harvesting is not a new technology but it has mostly been carried out on roofs. The water runs off a roof and is captured in gutters and downspouts. They then route the water into collection tanks. This is a fairly easy and sensible solution to dealing with water issues. While the water is not potable (drinkable), it can be used for things such as watering gardens or washing cars and driveways.

Water Isn't Wasted

Engineers have also come up with a new way to capture water runoff: masonry solutions. Permeable masonry materials include bricks or pavers. They can be laid for patios, walkways, or driveways without a traditional mortar used in the joints. Instead, small stones are used as filler between the pavers. That keeps them from shifting around. Traditionally, the mortar between pavers caused water to just run down the pathway or driveway and into the gutter. There, it is lost. However, the small stones allow water to soak down through the gaps between pavers. The rocks act as a natural filter. Leaves and other debris stay on top instead of running down under the pavers.

This area near Pleasanton in California, showing dry hills and a low reservoir, highlights the state's problem with drought.

The tiny stones between pavers in a pathway like this serve as an effective drainage tool.

ENGINEERING SOLUTIONS

Recently, RENCO USA won a building innovation award with its building system of interlocking molded blocks that look a whole lot like life-sized LEGO™ blocks. The bricks, however, are not made of clay or concrete. Instead, they are made of recycled glass fibers, resin, and stone. The composite building material, called mineral composite fiber reinforced (MCFR), is stronger than concrete. However, it is 75 percent lighter and can withstand a Category 5 hurricane. RENCO constructed its first apartment complex from MCFR blocks in 2023, in Palm Springs, Florida. Following color-coded building plans much like the instructions that come with a LEGO™ kit, 11 unskilled workers built the complex of three-story buildings in just eight weeks.

RENCO blocks could provide construction solutions in areas prone to hurricanes.

THE FUTURE IS EVOLVING

Engineers are creative problem-solvers. Through smart engineering solutions, building has evolved from the first simple tents of the hunter-gatherers to the gravity-defying skyscrapers of today. And exciting concepts are in the pipeline for the construction industry. It will continue to evolve in decades to come thanks to the work of building engineers.

Sustainable Buildings

The future of the building industry will continue to address sustainability concerns. Engineers are working to deal with the impacts of global climate change and sustainable building is key to that.

Another sustainability solution is using readily available building materials such as bamboo. Bamboo has a high tensile strength, which makes it good for construction. It also grows quickly and almost anywhere in the world.

Bamboo is both a sustainable and very strong building material.

Recycle and Upcycle

The building industry is also eager to use recycled materials wherever possible. In this book we have discussed several ways builders use recycled materials. However, the industry is constantly finding new ways to recycle or upcycle materials.

Recycled materials can be used in drywall, which is placed on walls and used to make ceilings.

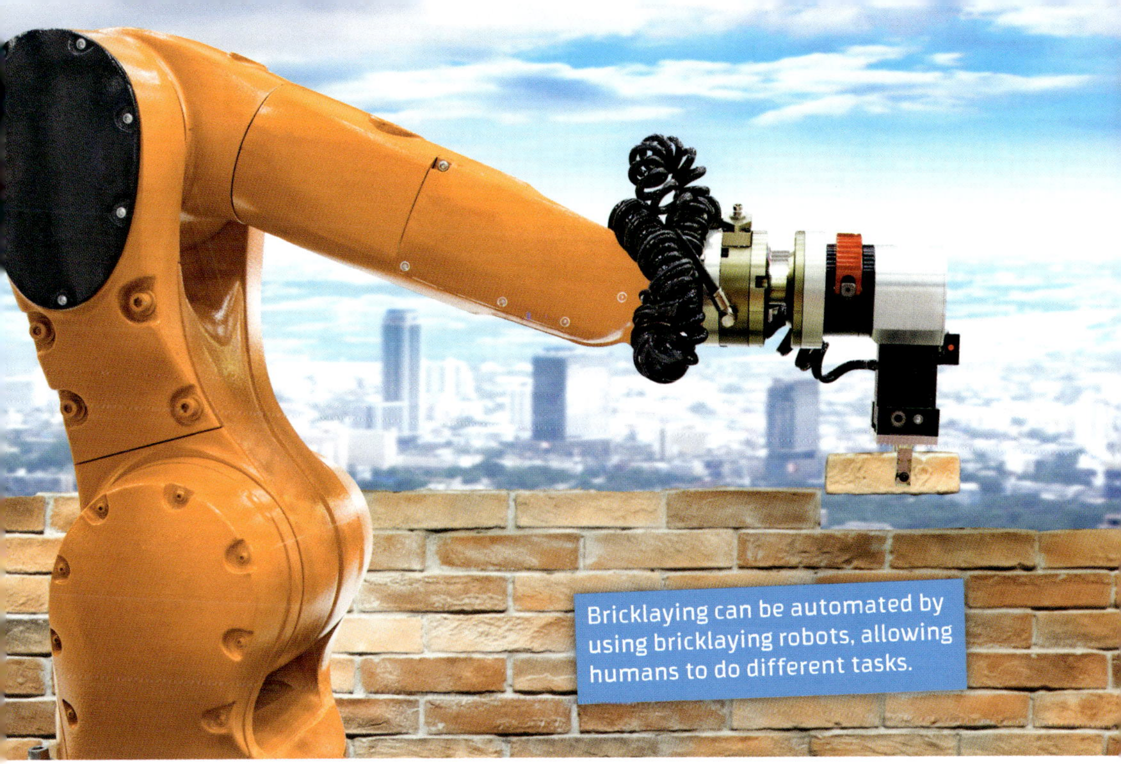

Bricklaying can be automated by using bricklaying robots, allowing humans to do different tasks.

Building Smarter

Another way the building industry is evolving is by collecting data through "smart" building materials. We have talked about smart bricks with sensors, but there are other parts of buildings that can also include sensors to track data. For example, new plumbing systems include sensors that can detect leaks or other potential issues with the pipes of a building.

Robotics and Automation

Robotics and automation are poised to revolutionize the building industry, too. There is some concern that the use of robotics will limit the number of jobs available to people. However, the upside to robots performing manual tasks is that it saves the wear and tear on workers' bodies. Lifting and transporting heavy construction materials and performing repetitive tasks such as bricklaying is hard work and tiring. So if people can work in other areas of the industry that are less physically tiring, using robots is a benefit.

EVOLVE AS AN ENGINEER

Intelligent engineering solutions require smart and creative brains. The amazing engineering minds of the past allowed us to move from tents made of animal skins and dazzling pyramids to towering skyscrapers. The exciting field of engineering can also be incredibly rewarding, particularly when you are a part of solutions that will benefit the planet. If you would like to build an engineering career, explore the following pages to discover how you could work in this ever-evolving field and help fix our building issues.

EVOLVING CAREERS IN ENGINEERING

For would-be engineers, there are many exciting job opportunities within the building industry. As this exciting engineering field develops, so too do the career options within it. Here are just some of the evolving engineering roles you could explore.

Architectural Engineer

Architectural engineers design and create buildings and other structures. They must have the creativity to design structures. They also need a solid knowledge of engineering principles to make sure those buildings will be safe and structurally sound. They work on everything from the initial design development to the final stages of construction and post-construction inspections and evaluation.

Civil Engineer

Like architectural engineers, civil engineers may work on buildings. However, they may also work on the design, construction, and maintenance of other infrastructure projects. They include roads, bridges, airports, and water supply systems. They are not focused on the look of a building, as architectural engineers may be. Instead, they focus on making sure that projects are safe and structurally sound.

Civil engineers look at building plans with an eye on structural integrity.

Electromechanical Engineer

If you are interested in the automation or robotics side of the building industry, you might be interested in electromechanical engineering. As the building industry moves more toward prefabrication and automation, more electromechanical engineers will be needed. They design and operate automation tools.

Environmental Engineer

Current building has a heavy focus on sustainability and environmentally friendly solutions, and environmental engineers are a valuable part of the team for that reason. Environmental engineers may assess building projects and sites for the environmental impact. They may also help design building systems that help protect the environment.

Environmental engineers are a critical part of the building team as we work toward a more sustainable future.

Materials Engineer

If you are interested in working on building at the materials level, you might be interested in materials engineering. Materials engineers create and study different types of materials. They try to find new substances that can be added to steel to strengthen it. Materials engineers work to solve problems in a variety of different engineering fields. They are involved whenever something needs to be broken down to the atomic level to address a problem and find a solution.

Mechanical Engineer

Mechanical engineers work in a lot of different areas. That is because their expertise enables them to design, develop, build, and maintain many types of mechanical and thermal sensor devices. As "smart" buildings are becoming more and more common, there's a great need for mechanical engineers in the building process. They also work on more traditional building structures, such as elevators and escalators.

How to Get into Engineering

If you think some or all of the roles outlined on the previous pages could be for you, the next steps in building a career in engineering start at school. Focus on STEM subjects because you will need qualifications in this area. STEM includes science, technology, engineering, and math. Engineers use math to problem solve and figure out designs, so it is an important skill to work on. Science is important too, because you'll need to understand physical science concepts such as forces, energy, and materials.

STEM Clubs and Camps

Consider joining a STEM club. This is a great place to work on your engineering skills. Many schools have clubs that focus on robotics, coding, and engineering challenges. Taking part will give you important hands-on experience that will help set you up for a career in engineering. You could also try a STEM camp. Many summer camps are STEM-focused today, to help young people develop these important skills. You can also explore the many STEM-focused online camps and classes available if you don't find an in-person one near you.

Consider Coding and Kits

Many areas of engineering require coding skills, so working on understanding the basics of coding is a great way to get into engineering. Try platforms such as Scratch, Python, or Blockly. Programming is very important in engineering fields such as robotics and electrical engineering. You can also work on simple projects such as games, apps, and easy robots to put what you have learned into practice. Having fun with kits can also help build your engineering skills. Try working with LEGO™, Arduino, and similar kits to build robots, electronic devices, and gadgets.

STEM and robotics clubs and camps are great places to get some hands-on engineering experience.

Any practical work like this will fire up your engineering brain and show you how exciting this area can be.

Talk to Other Engineers

Tell your teachers that you are interested in engineering, and they may be able to put you in touch with engineers who could talk to you about career options. You may even be able to visit engineers at work and see what a day in the life in this career is like. School counselors are also great people to talk to about career options, and they may be able to find engineering mentors for you to talk to. They will also be able to advise on courses to take once you finish school that will help put you on your path to a career in engineering.

Find Out More

When thinking about the next steps after school, spend time researching engineering programs at colleges and universities. The more you can find out now, the better placed you will be when the time comes to apply for a course.

There are different types of engineering, like mechanical, electrical, civil, aerospace, and environmental engineering. Each one leads to different kinds of jobs, so exploring your options early can help you decide what interests you most. Many colleges offer open days, online tours, and information sessions so you can see what their programs are like and ask questions.

GLOSSARY

aggregate a material formed from loosely crushed pieces of a substance
agricultural related to the science or practice of farming
alloy a metal that is made from two or more metallic elements
anchored held securely in position
archeologists people who study human history and prehistory
atomic related to atoms
atoms basic units of chemical elements
bacteria single-celled organisms that have cell walls but no organized nucleus
bedrock solid rock that lies under loose deposits such as soil
bioelectricity electrical currents generated by biological processes
blast furnace a type of furnace used to produce industrial metals, such as molten iron
brittle hard but easily breakable
carbon dioxide a colorless, odorless gas produced by burning carbon and organic compounds and by breathing
carbon footprint the total amount of greenhouse gas produced by a particular activity
cast-iron a hard, brittle alloy of iron and carbon
chutes sloping channels or passages through which things can pass
civilizations societies that have a particular culture and way of life
climate change shifts in temperature and weather patterns
climates general weather conditions of a given area
conveyer belt a continuously moving belt that moves objects from one place to another
corrodes damages or destroys by chemical action
deforest to clear an area of trees
domed shaped like a rounded vault
dowel a peg used to hold together pieces of a structure
drainage a means of removing extra water or liquid waste
drones remote-controlled aircraft or flying devices that have no pilot
drought a prolonged period of no or low rainfall
drywall a type of board that forms the interior walls of a structure; usually made from plaster, wood pulp, or other materials
durable able to withstand pressure or damage
dwellings places where people live
ecosystem a community of organisms that depend on each other, and their physical environment
efficient maximum productivity with minimum wasted effort or expense
elements parts of a whole
emissions substances released into the air
environmental relating to the natural world and the impact of human activity on it

environmentally conscious concerned with the environment and the impact of human activity on it

evidence facts or information that can support whether something is true

evolved developed gradually from a simple to a more complex form

excavate to make a hole by digging

finite having limits or bounds

fire-retardant something that can slow or stop the spread of fire

flammable easily catches fire

fossil fuels natural fuels, such as coal and gas, formed from the remains of living organisms

foundation the lowest load-bearing part of a building. Usually the base on which a building lies

foundry a factory for casting metal

global climate change overall change in climate patterns across the globe

greenhouse gases gases such as carbon dioxide that contribute to the warming of Earth's atmosphere

hoppers containers for bulk material such as rock. They typically have an opening so contents can be discharged through the bottom

humidity the amount of water vapor in the atmosphere

hunter-gatherers people who moved from place to place and hunted or fished for meat, and gathered plants for food

hydraulic presses mechanical devices that use the static pressure of a liquid to create a force

incline a sloped surface

infinite limitless in space or size

innovations new methods and ideas

Inuit Indigenous people from northern Canada, Greenland, and Alaska

irrigation the supply of water to land or crops

laminated manufactured by bonding layers of a material together

landfill waste waste products that are put in the landfill and do not decompose quickly

level a tool used to determine whether a surface is level

levers rigid bars that rest on pivots. Levers are used to move heavy loads with one end while pressure is applied to the other end of the lever

load-bearing in building, walls that support much of the weight of a building

logging cutting down of timber

lumber timber that has been processed into boards

manufacturing the making of items on a large scale using machinery

masonry a type of construction in which materials are connected using mortar or grout

masons stoneworkers

Mesopotamians an ancient civilization that existed in what is now Iraq between 600 and 400 BCE

Ming dynasty the dynasty that ruled China from 1368 to 1644 CE

molten liquified by heat

mortar a substance used to join pieces of stone or bricks to form a structure. Mortar is applied when it is wet and as it dries, it fixes surrounding materials into position

nanofibers fibers of material that are no more than a few nanometers (one nanometer equals one billionth of a meter) thick

natural resources materials or substances that occur in nature, such as minerals, forests, and water

oxygen a colorless, odorless gas that is essential to plant and animal life

permeable allowing liquids or gases to pass through

piles heavy beams or posts that are driven into a riverbed or soft ground to support a structure

polymer a substance with a molecular structure that consists mostly (or entirely) of a large number of similar units that are bonded together

porous having small spaces or holes through which air or liquid can pass

power grid a network of power transmission lines and distribution centers that carries electricity from power plants to consumers

prefabricated made beforehand in another area and then transported to be put together where needed

principles fundamental sources or bases of something

processed been through a series of mechanical or chemical operations to change or preserve it

pyramid a structure with a square or triangular base and sloping sides that meet in a point at the top

quarry to extract stones or other materials from an area called a quarry

recyclable able to be reused

sanitation conditions related to public health

satellites artificial bodies put in orbit around Earth

seismic related to earthquakes or other vibrations of the earth

sensors devices that detect or measure things in the environment

Seven Wonders of the Ancient World seven notable structures from between the eight century BCE and the fifth century CE. Only one is still standing: the Great Pyramid of Giza

sledges similar to sleds, vehicles on runners to carry passengers or loads of materials

stationary unmoving

Stone Age a prehistoric period when tools and weapons were made from stone or from bone, wood, or horn

structural engineering branch of civil engineering that deals with modern buildings and similar structures

sustainable able to be maintained at a certain rate or level

thermal mass a material's ability to absorb, store, and release heat

trowel a small handheld tool used to apply and spread mortar

FIND OUT MORE

Books

Castaldo, Nancy. *Buildings That Breathe: Greening the World's Cities.* Twenty-First Century Books, 2025.

Estes, Fred. *Teen Innovators: Nine Young People Engineering a Better World with Creative Inventions.* Zest Books, 2022.

McCauley, Paula. *Engineering for Teens: A Beginner Book for Aspiring Engineers.* Callisto Teens, 2021.

Small, Cathleen. *How to Choose Your Perfect Engineering Career* (STEM Career Choices). Cheriton Children's Books, 2023.

Websites

Read more about the history of construction at:
https://constructible.trimble.com/construction-industry/a-very-brief-history-of-the-construction-industry

Find out more about construction engineering at:
www.indeed.com/career-advice/finding-a-job/what-is-construction-engineering

Tinker Cad is a free web application that allows you to explore 3D design, electronics, and coding to complete many exciting projects. Find out more at:
www.tinkercad.com

Publisher's note to educators and parents:
All the websites featured above have been carefully reviewed to ensure that they are suitable for students. However, many websites change often, and we cannot guarantee that a site's future contents will continue to meet our high standards of educational value. Please be advised that students should be closely monitored whenever they access the Internet.

INDEX

ABOUT THE AUTHORS

Sarah Eason and Cathleen Small have written a wide variety of books for teens, including many STEM titles.